D1300112

ALL OF BABA'S GREAT GRANDCHILDREN

ETHNIC IDENTITY IN THE NEXT CANADA

The MOHYLA LECTURE SERIES is a programme of annual lectures
devoted to a discussion of Ukrainian heritage and current affairs. The 1999
Mohyla Lecture was delivered by Myrna Kostash, November 19, 1999 at
the Great Hall, Shannon Library, St. Thomas More College,
University of Saskatchewan.

A MOHYLA LECTURE PUBLICATION
Nationbuilding Series No. 1

SERIES EDITOR
BOHDAN S. KORDAN

Canadian Cataloguing in Publication Data

Kostash, Myrna
All of Baba's great grandchildren

(Mohyla lectures. Nationbuilding series; no. 1)
Copublished by: Prairie Centre for the Study of Ukrainian Heritage.
ISBN 0-88880-420-2

1.Ukrainian Canadians—Ethnic identity. I. Prairie Centre for the Study of
Ukrainian Heritage. II. Title. III. Series
FC106.U5K682 2000   971'.00491791   C00-911459-9
F1080.U5k672 2000

Publication of this volume was made possible by a grant from the
Millennium Bureau of Canada

© Myrna Kostash
HERITAGE PRESS
Prairie Centre for the Study of Ukrainian Heritage
St. Thomas More College, University of Saskatchewan
Saskatoon, Saskatchewan Canada S7N 0W6

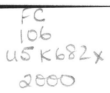

ALL OF BABA'S
GREAT GRANDCHILDREN

ETHNIC IDENTITY IN THE NEXT CANADA

MYRNA KOSTASH

HERITAGE PRESS
2000

Beyond Identity Politics

Some years ago, in the magazine *Books in Canada*, writer Barry Callaghan described his father Morley Callaghan's literary effort to "set down the language of the place [Toronto in the '20s and '30s]," to "clear" it the same way Canadian homesteaders had cleared the land.[1] He confessed to his interviewer that he just didn't know "what's going on here any more."

Don't get him wrong, he hastened to add, this wasn't about being mean-spirited, but "it does not fill me with a sense of exhilaration and alertness about my own place, and the language of my own place, that Rohinton Mistry is here in Canada, writing about India, in the language that is appropriate to India." Callaghan felt estranged from a lot of current literature: "It seems awfully strange that we should find ourselves...beaming under the umbrella of multiculturalism, embracing colonial voices as if they were our own."

I remember that I was both cheered and discomforted by Callaghan's argument. Cheered, because I remembered with nostalgic fondness the excited discussions that took place in Alberta in the late 1970s and early 1980s among artists and writers of my generation, about the burgeoning production of "our" stories — by which we meant the literature of Margaret Laurence and Robert Kroetsch, Rudy Wiebe and Andy Suknaski, and all the others who had broken the colonial bonds with Britain, New York and Toronto, to write about who and where we were right now, deeply rooted historically, sociologically and psychically in the Canadian prairie — a discussion that has since been overtaken by history, not to say theory.

But I was also discomforted, because even then there was something unattractive about Callaghan's querulous remarks, something unimaginative, out

of date, quaint, not to the point anymore. Everything has been problematized, as the theorists say,
opened and exposed to the gaze of Canadians
whose view of things wasn't canvassed when we
first circulated such comfortable notions as "place"
and "here," not to mention "our own."

Whose is that exactly? Is it more my grand-
mother's than yours? Do we all agree what "here"
looks like? Is it old or new, empty or full, wild or
urban? How on earth is a language that's been
composed in Mississauga "appropriate to India"?
Are some English languages more Canadian than
others? Does Callaghan really mean that, if you're
"ethnic" ("an umbrella of multiculturalism"), you
live here as some kind of Displaced Person, the
flotsam and jetsam of offshore imperial holdings?
…And even "clearing the land" has a funny ring
to it these days.

Now I set the Callaghan interview alongside an
essay in an art catalogue by Henry Tsang. Tsang

wrote to introduce the artists in an exhibit, *Self Not Whole*, in Vancouver, that explored the idea of being Chinese. Chineseness, it turns out, is not easy to pin down; what the exhibition artists have in common, writes Tsang, is that "this term *Chinese* is vague, floating, and perhaps undefinable." Certainly, there are annual festivities and rituals that bring the community together but artist Heesok Chang, for instance, isn't even sure there is such a thing as a single Chinese "community"— so what do Chinese-Canadians mean when they say "we"? What do they mean when they say "white culture" as though they were completely outside it? Karin Lee wants to deconstruct the idea of the "ethnic," that undifferentiated person who lives in some vague place called the "margin." But she also wants to challenge the alternative — the conservative Chinese-Canadian retreat into traditional culture.

In *FUSE* magazine, two cultural activists in the South Asian communities of Toronto, looking back on their long experience in community organization, want us to think about whether "reliance on [ethnic] community" and personal identity are a sound basis for political organizing. Cultural boundaries between groups can become "entrenched," even racial. They can concretize the very difficulty they were meant to overcome — ghettoization — by foreclosing on "the possibility of cultural transformation, the reconstitution of community."[2]

So, in spite of Barry Callaghan's fears, the language of the above-mentioned artists *is* the language of "here," in all its hyphenation, its ambivalence, its confrontation, and its restless exploration of the possibility of belonging to a place they themselves are in the process of redefining.

I n 1995, sixty-eight percent of Canadians agreed with the observation that "on the whole, immigration is a good thing for Canada."[3] The 1998 Annual Poll published by *Maclean's* magazine did not even include a question about attitudes to multiculturalism and immigration. We Canadians seem to be *living* multiculturalism as though it were a normal, if not in fact a defining, characteristic of our collective identity. We Canadians have in fact agreed for some time that we live with both group and individual rights: the Official Languages Act, the separate school boards, the Indian Act (or, where superceded, Aboriginal land claims) as well as the Charter of Rights and Freedoms. We have agreed that groups as well as individuals need to express what is particular about themselves without jeopardizing their social and economic opportunity in "mainstream" society.[4]

After two years of conversation with 20-and 30-somethings, I come to the conclusion that they are a generation for whom the public self-expression of cultural minorities in no way contradicts the hope for expanded freedom and dignity in society as a whole. They may even say that minority self-expression is a condition of our collective dignity.

I began my conversations among Ukrainian-Canadians, the ones right across the street, in fact, Orysia Boychuk and her husband Volodymyr, residents, like I, in Hromada Housing Co-op, who had met while selling *pyrohy* at the Ukrainian Students' Club at the University of Alberta. Later I spoke with their friend Lisa McDonald, half-Ukrainian, half-French-Scottish.

Who are the Ukrainian-Canadians who come after me, after deficit slashing and program extermination, after webnets and the Coca-Colonization of everything, after Ukrainian independence and *Koka-Kola* in the sidewalk cafes of Kyiv? How does one go on being Ukrainian-Canadian in *their* world? Does it still matter, in the so-called global village, that hyphen is a kind of hinge between two equally compelling identities?

To answer No, it doesn't matter, would mean a radical excavation of the self, for both Orysia and Volodymyr were deeply imprinted by a politicization that took hold in childhood — Orysia in the Ukrainian-Canadian organizations in Oshawa, Ontario, and Volodymyr in the Soviet Ukrainian institutions of the USSR.

The several waves of Ukrainian immigration to Canada have each contributed to this institutionalization — and produced Orysia, in *sadochok*, in Saturday School (language and history and dance lessons), in Sunday School in St. George's Ukrainian Catholic Church, youth groups and summer camps, not to mention speaking Ukrainian at home. Meanwhile, Volodymyr made the long march through Young October, Young Pioneers and Komsomol groups. In the late 1980s, he launched into the most unforgettable years of his young life: the Gorbachevian experiment, *perebudova*, the political and social opening up of the Soviet collective.

To hear the list of their community activities — some twenty hours a week — is to wish them both a sabbatical: Ukrainian Professional and Business Club, Ukrainian Media Initiative, Verkhovyna Choir, Ukrainian Soccer Club and Ukrainian Canadian Congress — most of which are creatures of the multicultural Golden Age of the 1970s and early 1980s. "Everything I'm involved in is Ukrainian," Orysia observed, "but as I get older I think about being involved in something that is not Ukrainian. There are times when I've felt over-Ukrainianized, when I've wanted friends who are non-Ukrainians."

She had grown up when Ukraine was still a "captured" nation within the USSR. Crucial to the Ukrainian-Canadian community in which she was raised was that the Canadian-born generations should not be lost, that the struggle for independence not be betrayed by the fecklessness of Westernized youth whose sense of purpose no longer bent to the needs of the groaning motherland. The overriding mission of the diaspora Ukrainians was to *remember*, to be the rememberers of a people whose own texts were systematically erased by terror, violence, and sheer, grinding Russification.

Take Volodymyr, growing up in western Ukraine with no connection to Canada, and just as well: those with Canadian family were considered to be related to enemies of the people. When he finally visited Canada in 1991 and discovered the Ukrainian community in Edmonton, it brought tears to his eyes to hear kids — with first names like Kevin and Tracy and Grant — recite Taras Shevchenko.

And so, with independence in 1991, Ukraine finally became what its scattered generations had prayed for: normal. One could go visit, openly and garrulously, and for the first time in decades have normal human contact with real Ukrainians. And so off they went. McDonald went in 1993 to a youth camp north of Kyiv. "Army barracks, no flush toilets, people wearing the same clothes for weeks, and the same food day after day. Not at all like *my* camp experience in Canada with my blow dryer and ghetto blaster! And then we went to *dido's* village: it was so small and poor it didn't even have a road. People in clothes worn paper-thin, barefoot. We bought a kubassa for what a teacher makes in a month." From the horror stories of the Soviet era, she was prepared for the odiferous toilets, the irradiated orchards, the queues for scrawny chickens. "What I wasn't prepared for was the Seagram's boutique and the tortellini for lunch while the city of Lviv runs out of hot water in the afternoon."

Volodymyr was shocked by the social as well as economic back-sliding of his family: a mother now on pension (eighteen dollars a month) and father, once a professional truck driver, now paid in potatoes, and bartering in the local marketplace for goods. "If we never go back," Orysia summarized, "it's okay with me."

The implication of this disappointment is clear: emotional and intellectual resources not invested in Ukraine are freed up for Canada. According to Volodko, "The question now is what we're going to make of ourselves here, as Ukrainian-Canadians." Their duality is important, that residual "otherness" that every Canadian carries as baggage from ancestral cultures, even after the Mother Country has ceased to be a direct source of identity. In her dance classes with very young Ukrainian-Canadians, McDonald sees that maybe six out of thirty children are able to have a conversation in rudimentary Ukrainian and "making a *paska* is totally foreign to them. They've never been to church for the blessing of the *paska*, but they're dancing. Some part of them wants to, something in them wants to show that they're Ukrainian."

And, with this consciousness, the hyphenated Ukrainian-Canadian still has issues that implicate the rest of Canadian society. Among my interviewees, these include official acknowledgment of the 1914-1920 internment of over 5000 "enemy aliens," a perhaps not surprisingly lively topic for a generation reared on the campaigns for human rights in Ukraine, and who now want to "expand public memory so as to encompass [the internees'] suffering," as the sympathizing journalist, Mark Abley, wrote in the *Montreal Gazette* [February 22 1998]. Orysia Boychuk repeated this theme, that "a lot of issues relating to Ukrainian-Canadians get put on the back burner."

Invisibility. Marginality. A note of grievance entered the discussion. Ukrainians denied equal opportunities...their historical experience denied ...controversies about Holocaust Museums that engage all of Canadians, but when the Ukrainian-Canadian community erected a memorial to the dead of the 1933 Famine in Soviet Ukraine, for example, there were fellow citizens who denounced it as "anti-Soviet propaganda."

Another urgent inter-communal issue for these young people is the handling of the war crimes controversy, namely the intention of the Canadian government to deport suspected war criminals to Ukraine on grounds, not of evidence of war crimes, but of fraudulent entry into Canada after the Second World War. The Ukrainian-Canadian Students' Union [SUSK] has taken a position on this: "SUSK believes that all acts which violate the Canadian Criminal Code committed by Canadian citizens must be tried in Canada...SUSK categorically opposes the Canadian Department of Justice's use of denaturalization and deportation of Canadian citizens as a means of bringing war criminals to justice."

The vehemence with which Lisa McDonald defended this position is a reflection of her generation's bewilderment about the meaning of their grandparents' war: "Why aren't they [war crimes prosecutors] going after the Germans? That's what confuses me. So much stuff happened then, in any war so many bad things, things I can't even begin to imagine they went through, the things they would have had to do just to survive in such dire circumstances. I feel no guilt about Jews, that's a non-issue. Live and let live. This is a small world." Perhaps more acutely shaped by that war's effects in the Soviet Union, Volodymyr Boychuk emphasized there was no collective "we" who perpetrated crimes but "that man and that one and that one. And yes they are guilty. But we let ourselves get spit in the face all the time."

History, memory, trauma, the difficulty of recuperating history, the erasure of the past during the Soviet years: these are children of the loss of memory. I was rather taken back by their passions aroused by this issue of their marginalization. But until Ukrainian experience and articulation circulate in Canadian society, along with other narratives of displacement and discrimination, then even these twenty-first century Ukrainian-Canadians are still relegated to the margins of Canadian concern where their stories are confined in private memory and important only to them.

This is perhaps an extreme argument. After all, performances of Ukrainian dancing are very popular with general audiences, the giant *Pysanka* in Vegreville, Alberta, is a tourist attraction, and Sunshine Records of Winnipeg distributes over fifty titles in the category, "Baba's Records." But this sort of representation of Ukrainian-Canadian ethnicity increasingly disconcerts those born several generations down the line from the Galician pioneers of western Canada.

> *How are we presenting ourselves to one another and to the communities that are Canada? I don't think the average Ukrainian woman walking through the village or town is carrying bread and salt, or dancing to the kolomeyka, but for some reason there she is, 3 generations and a continent away, kicking up her heels on stages across the prairies.[...]Far from the urban reality of the aboriginal, multi-racial and multiethnic populations of Canadian cities where most of us live and work, the festival community is a temporary space[...]it is a suspended reality where we indulge in the fantasy of a coherent Ukrainian-Canadian place.*

> Mary Anne Charney
> "Making Sense of Pysanka:
> Is This What Ukrainian Culture Is All About?"
> *Zdorov*, Summer 1998

Taking up the challenge of representation is Nestor Gula in Toronto, 30-something editor of an English-language magazine, *Zdorov*, (mainly) for Ukrainian-Canadians. Having studied magazine journalism at Ryerson Journalism School, having worked at a Ukrainian newspaper in 1993 in a Partners for Progress program, having turned down the "opportunity" to work in Ukraine again in 1994 —"been there, done that…all you do is sit around and drink"— Gula decided that the audience he wanted to address was…himself. The young Ukrainian-Canadian trapped in a love-hate relationship with the Old Country, one minute bashing away at its "financial crisis, sick people, poor people, government in crisis, law on privatization passed on Monday, canceled on Tuesday, repassed on Wednesday…yadda, yadda, yadda," the next minute cheering on the Ukrainian athletes at the Olympics, "Let's go, Ukraine!"

Gula cheerfully admitted in an interview with me that he also plays on the "guilt" of the forty- and fifty-somethings who know they *should* be speaking more Ukrainian and buying their own subscription to *Ukrainian Weekly* and sending more money over to Ukraine but who are really mainly interested in the doings of their own community — the arts, celebrities, travel, food, lore, opinion. When I asked him how he wanted to represent Ukrainians in his magazine, Gula answered: "Normal. Even cool. You can be a Ukrainian and doing something cool as opposed to being a doctor, dentist, lawyer."

The model for this kind of journalism was the very cool *Eyetalian* magazine, also published in Toronto, with *Globe&Mail* columnists and a Governor General's Award-winning novelist as contributors, a very snazzy lay-out, sumptuous ads for *trattorias* on College Street and holidays in Tuscany. "Right there you have a problem," I challenged Gula. "Italians think it's really cool being Italian and going to Italy and listening to opera, and the rest of the world thinks so too. For Canadians, Italy is the Roman Empire, the Renaissance, the source of civilization, while Ukraine?" I let the question hang in the air. Gula nodded in agreement. "They think of us as dancers."

But when I interviewed the editor of *Eyetalian*, John Montesano, I stood corrected about Italian "cool." Montesano reminded me that thirty years ago Italians, especially those from the south, were the "black" immigrants of 1950s Canada. "You come in, do the crappy jobs, then they shit on you for taking away the jobs. In their heart of hearts, what do the Anglos think of us?" Montesano argued that "Italian chic" is limited to the "white" part of Italy, the north. Tourists don't go to his part of Italy, Calabria: "It's too dark." When we say we love Italian culture, we're not talking about *his* culture. We wouldn't last two hours in Calabria. "Calabrians are strange, they look at you really mean. Anglos' sense of Italianness is very narrowly defined. You have to get past hanging out on College Street and ordering arugula salad."

But Montesano admitted that *everybody's* view of Italianness, including his own, is shaped by the mass media, and he told a funny story on himself. How he grew up in Downsview, a Toronto suburb, and never spent time on College, the original main street of the Italian immigrant community, until his non-Italian friends from York University began hanging out there. That's how he learned what bruschetta is. Pronounced: *brusketa*. "They'd ask me if I wanted to order some *bruschetta*. I'd correct their pronunciation with pride: Hey, get the language right. But I didn't know what the heck it was. You know what it is? Bread with tomatoes spread on it. Well, we ate that at home but we never called it that. Never put it on a plate with little parsley flakes. What the hell is that? We got a piece of bread, put some olive oil and chopped some tomatoes on it and ate it."

I bought copies of both *Zdorov* and *Eyetalian* and made a comparison of their Spring 1998 contents. *Letters to the Editor* carried the usual complaints from readers that the respective magazine's writers had gravely misrepresented the correspondent's community, whether in "making fun of our [Ukrainian-Canadian] incompetencies" or making "hackneyed criticisms" of the Italian Catholic Church. Older generations have generally disapproved of exposures of dirty laundry to the "English," preferring what John Montesano called the "we're Italian, rah, rah, rah syndrome," even when the community's short-comings are well-known. Nestor Gula at *Zdorov* ran a piece about wife abuse among Ukrainian-Canadians, and got "zero reaction" from a community presumably in deep denial.

Both magazines ran first-person exposés of the language policing among generations. A reader of *Eyetalian* wrote a letter to the editor: "*Now, speaking Italian seems to have contained in it a form of unspoken competition between us first and second-*

*generation Italian-Canadians for membership into
something, as though whoever can speak it best, has
the right accent, knows the right words, uses the correct grammar, is the most authentic among us, truer
to that which is Italian in us, an outward marker of
knowing one's own self."*

A *Zdorov* commentary ran: *"The [annual] meeting was conducted almost entirely in Ukrainian...
One woman stood up and sneered [at an English-
speaking speaker], 'I didn't understand a word you
said. Speak Ukrainian.' Excuse me? You've been in
this country forty-plus years and you can't understand a few, simple words in English?...No, better
some yolop [imbecile] who speaks perfect Ukrainian
than an English-speaking person who can actually
contribute valuable knowledge and experience."*

Typical of the ethnic press are the short news
stories about notable personalities usually over-
looked by the non-ethnic media — the fundraiser,
the folk musician, the small human interest stories,

and the culinary features about recipes and, in the case of *Eyetalian*, the restaurants, in the case of *Zdorov*, humour: "Ten reasons why *varenyky* are better than sex."

But the publications are only superficially alike. Subtext is all, and with respect to Ukrainians and Italians living in Toronto, the sub-texts drive the real meaning of the magazines' intervention in the media marketplace.

Take the advertising, for example, as much signifying of hyper-urban design smarts and nuovo Tuscan chic in *Eyetalian* as of ethnic ghettoization and unvarnished folksiness in *Zdorov*. When I remarked to Montesano that the design, lay-out, colour of his magazine "flattered the non-Italians' view of Italians," far removed from stereotyped *paisani* in impoverished, Mafia-ridden Sicilian villages, he admitted he was trying to communicate with a certain demographic, to connect readers back to the city. "There are tens of thousands like me. We don't speak standard Italian, don't identify with Italian institutions, like the Columbus Centre, or Giovanni Caboto and all that crap, and don't go to church." Psychologically secure as urban Canadians, his generation is in a position to "take control over how our identity is being represented," and for the moment, at least, this sophisticated identity of the Italian-Canadian at ease in the upscale *trattoria* and furniture shops of the metropolis coincides with non-Italian views of the community.

By contrast, Ukrainian-Canadians still generally go along with the popular view of themselves as colourful, dancing, *horilka*-tippling hunkies recently arrived from a wheat farm in Saskatchewan. Witness the humourous treatment in *Zdorov* of Ukrainian behavioural stereotypes ("When attending services in the church of your choice, do you: sit in the basement and smoke? Score 4 points"), the popularity of Florida as a holiday destination, cuisine (usually the food that *baba* cooked, *not*

Chicken Kiev). There is an uneasy relationship between this genial jokiness and the intention of *Zdorov* to air serious issues of Ukrainian-Canadian belonging to the wider Canadian community. The strategy seems to be to highlight the "good news" of Ukrainian-Canadian achievement in the arts, science and business, and to walk softly around more provocative issues, such as the under-representation of Ukrainian-Canadians in the Canadian elites, and the pursuit of alleged war criminals by Canadian courts.

Although Gula had targeted the "yuppies" of Toronto as his "demographic," with their expensive cars, golf club memberships and monster houses in the suburbs, he knows he treads a fine line between what's "interesting" about Ukrainian-Canadians and what's "negative," and what his potential readership is ready to accept as its representation. Understandably, Gula may have to be at least half-attuned to the readers who, unpersuaded by the editorial pitch to be "cool Ukes," complained that the mother of a profiled celebrity was German, not Ukrainian. "The same people will say we should run Gretzky on the cover. When I point out he's not Ukrainian, they say, 'Well, if you put him on the cover, people will think he is!'"

There's no getting around the psychological *insecurity* of a community that has periodically lived under a cloud in Canada as "enemy aliens" in the Great War, "Reds" in the 1930s, anti-Communist extremists in the 1950s, and aging, anti-Semitic alleged pro-Nazi collaborators in the 1980s and 1990s. Compared to these stigmatizations, the fun-loving bumpkin is almost lovable.

"Theory" reminds us not to confuse the ideal of commonality with the assumption that we therefore live in community, blissfully ignorant of the multiplicity and instability that complicate any given group's identity.

Knowing Ourselves

At a conference at York University in 1997 in which I participated, "Multiculturalism in Canada: A Dialogue for the 21st Century," the Black Canadian writer Dionne Brand said this (I cite from notes): "Official culture thinks immigrants should be emptied of their past. This is undesirable. [What is desirable is that] stories join other stories to become part of the collectivity. I resist the idea that the collectivity is a done deal that cannot be added to or changed." When immigrants and other hybrids decide to open up their communities to a *sharing* of stories and histories, and to participation in civil society, then the popular charge that hyphenated Canadians are "about" ghettoization, exoticism, and separatism is simply hysterical.

Yet official multiculturalism policy has been vigorously disputed by those who see it as an accommodation with the fragmenting tendency of the post-modern world, a systematic deconstruction of a whole and unified concept of a place called Canada, to which we all belong in the same relationship as our neighbours.

But such a Canada is in fact impossible, as our philosophers will be quick to instruct us. We are so diverse in our ethnicities and religions, national origins and languages, diverse even in number of generations resident on the continent, that any one Canadian's ideal of Canada will be contested from all sides because it bears only imperfect resemblance to the ideal of the Canadian sitting beside her on the bus.

In just such a way has "Canada" always known itself. We know ourselves as Canadians by the constant encounter and engagement with just-arrived "otherness." The new otherness inevitably wobbles old certainties about who we "really" are, and how our constituent cultural diversity is to be integrated into something called the "national" life. This is never resolved by any particular generation once and for all. As is so clear from my interviewees, each new generation of Canadians has to think through its own relationship to the past and to its own civic desires.

"Theory" reminds us not to confuse the ideal of commonality with the assumption that we therefore live in community, blissfully ignorant of the multiplicity and instability that complicate any given group's identity. We are all being challenged to come up with a language that may be employed persuasively in the public sphere, which is where our *collective* if not common interests coincide — a collective interest in cultural diversity, for instance, or in social justice.[5]

A hopeful perspective on this post-modern moment is provided by the British Ghanian artist,

Kobena Mercer, interviewed in the Canadian magazine *Fuse*, who sees "a moment of reconciliation," not erasure, in cultural mixing, who sees a certain kind of "cultural competence" in a society that is interested in how ethnic difference can be brought into the "common culture."[6]

We who have been several generations now in Canada, for all the uncompleted business of our communal life, are being invited, I think, by the new strangers at our gates, to engage in a politics of resemblance.

The compulsion to tell falls on the next generation, and the next, until it will be heard, or heard again, as though for the first time.

The Next Generation

Let us conclude, then, with our artists, for a Ukrainian-Canadian self that does not erase *baba* and *dido* but refigures them in the new cultural materials handed to a new generation. Back in 1993, the videographer, film-maker and writer Marusia Bociurkiw, after years of "disowning" her ethnic baggage, returned to it in a passionate essay in which she confessed that, up to now, she did not feel she had "permission" to look at where she came from ethnically. The permission had been withheld not only by non-Ukrainian indifference, perhaps even hostility, but by the silences within her own family, the "unspoken history of my parents' immigration [...] so traumatic in its import that my Baba, still, 60 years later, tells and retells her ocean crossing story in incredible detail, to anyone who'll listen."[7]

The compulsion to tell falls on the next generation, and the next, until it will be heard, or heard again, as though for the first time. In 1996, artist Tanya Rusnak exhibited her multi-media installation, *O Emigratsii* (*On Emigration*), which she described in the catalogue as a "recovery project — a work of preservation […] an effort to reconstruct, elevate and preserve the fallen signs, symbols, broken narratives and persisting words of early Ukrainian immigrants." They persist for her, great-grandchild poking around in the debris of the emptied settlements in north-eastern Alberta, excavating grains, lumps of coal, flour, dried mud, onions, beeswax candles. On wooden boxes she literally reinscribes the code words of the missing narrative: VILLAGE, HUNGER, NEW LAND, PERISH. On the wall above the boxes she hung, like so many gravestones, small panels decorated with traces of photographs, Cyrillic lettering, withered sunflowers. Death, rot, decay…but not quite.

She has retrieved them, handled them, reordered them, and made us look again.

The repressed will always return. Because, half-knowingly perhaps, we have passed it on.

NOTES:

1 "The Impassioned Exile of Barry Callaghan," Roger Burford Mason, interviewer, *Books in Canada*, Vol 22, No. 5 (Summer 1993), pp. 9-13

2 Sean Lokaisingh-Meighoo and Arif Noorani, "Some Keywords and Arguments in Cultural Politics," *FUSE*, Vol. 22, Number 2.

3 Reginald W. Bibby, *The Bibby Report: Social Trends Canadian Style*, (Toronto: Stoddart, 1995).

4 W. Kymlicka, *Multicultural Citizenship* (Oxford: Clarendon Press, 1995).

5 This point was made by writer Heather Menzies at the 1997 Writers' Union of Canada Annual General Meeting, as reported in the Union's *Newsletter*, Vol. 25, Number 3.

6 *FUSE*, Vol. 20, Number 4.

7 *Canadian Women's Studies*, Vol. 14, Number 1.

MYRNA KOSTASH is the author of *All of Baba's Children* (1977), *Bloodlines: A Journey Into Eastern Europe* (1993), *The Doomed Bridegroom: A Memoir* (1998) and *The Next Canada: In Search of the Future Nation* (2000). She has been Max Bell Professor of Journalism at the University of Regina, Ashley Fellow at Trent University, and in 1993-94 served as Chair of The Writer's Union of Canada.

Two hundred and fifty copies of this book were set in ITC Berkeley, drawn by Tony Stan and issued in 1983. It is a revision of Frederic Goudy's 1938 University of California Oldstyle, and considered one of Goudy's masterpieces. Produced by the Heritage Press.

Designed by Edison del Canto
Printed and bound by Houghton Boston
Saskatoon, Saskatchewan
Canada